Spectacular Sports

Bowling

Decomposing Numbers 1–10

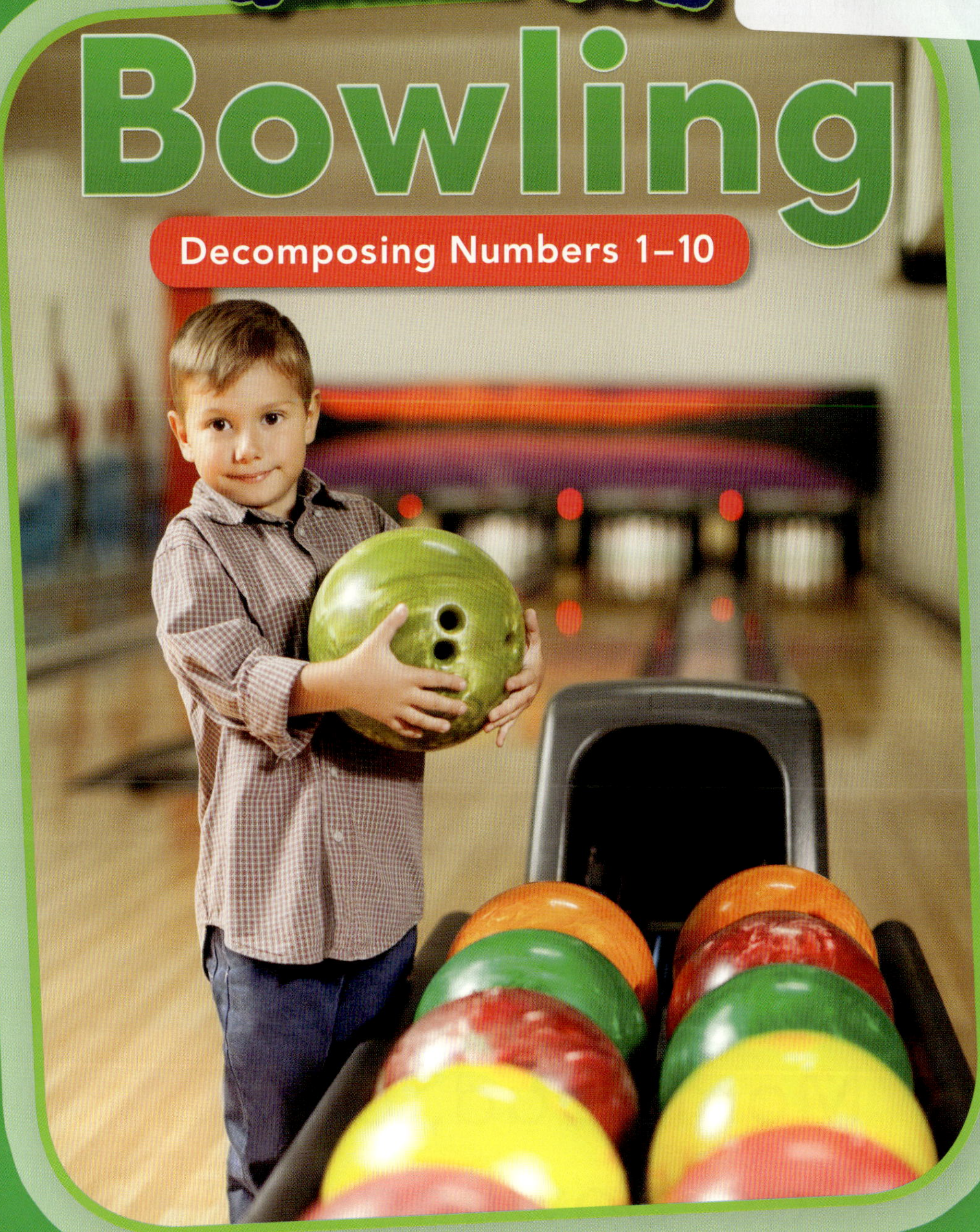

Linda Claire

Mom, Dad, and
I go bowling.

It is fun!

There are 10 pins.

There is 1 ball.

I bowl first.

I throw the ball.

2 pins go down!

8 pins are left.

It is still my turn.

I throw the ball again.

5 pins go down!

3 pins are left.

The pins go
up again.

I throw the
ball. Strike!

Problem Solving

It is Dad's turn to bowl. He gets 2 chances to throw the ball. How many ways can he knock down 10 pins? Use objects or draw pictures to show different ways.

Answer Key

Answers will vary.
Examples:

3 pins and 7 pins;
5 pins and 5 pins;
7 pins and 3 pins

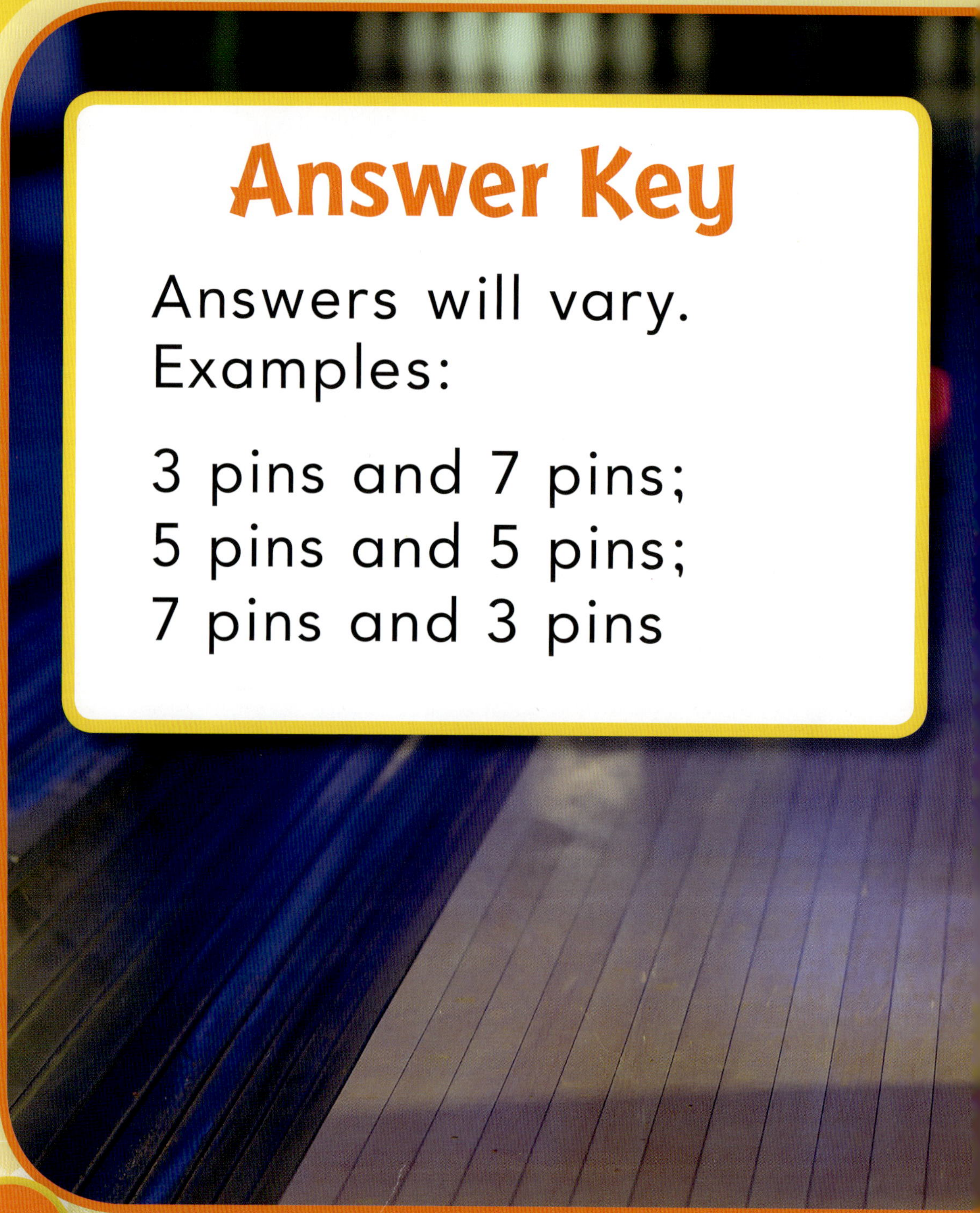

Consultants

Nicole Belasco, M.Ed.
Kindergarten Teacher, Colonial School District

Colleen Pollitt, M.A.Ed.
Math Support Teacher, Howard County Public Schools

Publishing Credits

Rachelle Cracchiolo, M.S.Ed., *Publisher*
Conni Medina, M.A.Ed., *Managing Editor*
Dona Herweck Rice, *Series Developer*
Emily R. Smith, M.A.Ed., *Series Developer*
Diana Kenney, M.A.Ed., NBCT, *Content Director*
June Kikuchi, *Content Director*
Véronique Bos, *Creative Director*
Robin Erickson, *Art Director*
Stacy Monsman, M.A., and Karen Malaska, M.Ed., *Editors*
Michelle Jovin, M.A., *Associate Editor*
Fabiola Sepulveda, *Graphic Designer*

Image Credits: All images from iStock and/or Shutterstock.

Library of Congress Cataloging-in-Publication Data

Names: Claire, Linda, author.
Title: Spectacular sports : bowling / Linda Claire.
Description: Huntington Beach, CA : Teacher Created Materials Inc., [2019] | Audience: K to Grade 3.
Identifiers: LCCN 2017059890 (print) | LCCN 2018010929 (ebook) | ISBN 9781480759626 (e-book) | ISBN 9781425856243 (pbk.)
Subjects: LCSH: Bowling--Juvenile literature. | Counting--Juvenile literature.
Classification: LCC GV903.5 (ebook) | LCC GV903.5 .C55 2019 (print) | DDC 796.358/22--dc23
LC record available at https://lccn.loc.gov/2017059890

Teacher Created Materials
5301 Oceanus Drive
Huntington Beach, CA 92649-1030
www.tcmpub.com

ISBN 978-1-4258-5624-3

Printed in Malaysia. Thumbprints.44180